Copyright © 2023 Pen Paper Canvas

All rights reserved. No part of this book, including the artwork, may be reproduced or transmitted in any form or by any means, electronic or mechanical, including photocopying, recording, or by any information storage and retrieval system, without written permission from the author, except for the inclusion of brief quotations in a review. Requests for permission should be addressed to Pen Paper Canvas at connect@penpapercanvas.com.

This book is a work of non-fiction, but names and identifying details of people, places, and events have been changed to protect their privacy and confidentiality. Any resemblance to actual persons, living or dead, events, or locales is entirely coincidental.

Thank you for respecting the author's efforts to protect the privacy and confidentiality of those involved in the events recounted in this book.

Chaos to Clarity

Mandala

A circular geometric design that is used as a spiritual symbol in Hinduism and Buddhism. Mandalas are used as a form of meditation and as a way to focus the mind, as well as a form of art therapy. They can be created with different shapes and colors, and they can have different meanings depending on the culture and context in which they are used.

Want FREE coloring pages and journaling prompts sent to you every month? Join the Pen Paper Canvas Club for free here: www.penpapercanvas.com/ppcclub.

As I created this book, I was 26 years old and had recently quit my job to pursue the dream of becoming an author and businesswoman. It would mean the world to me if you could leave a review on Amazon. Your feedback will help me improve and grow as an artist. Thank you so much for your support!

Color Swatch

Use this page to test different art mediums. We suggest using dry mediums such as colored pencils, pastels, and crayons. If you use ink-based tools such as pens or markers, please place a printer page behind the design to prevent bleeding through.

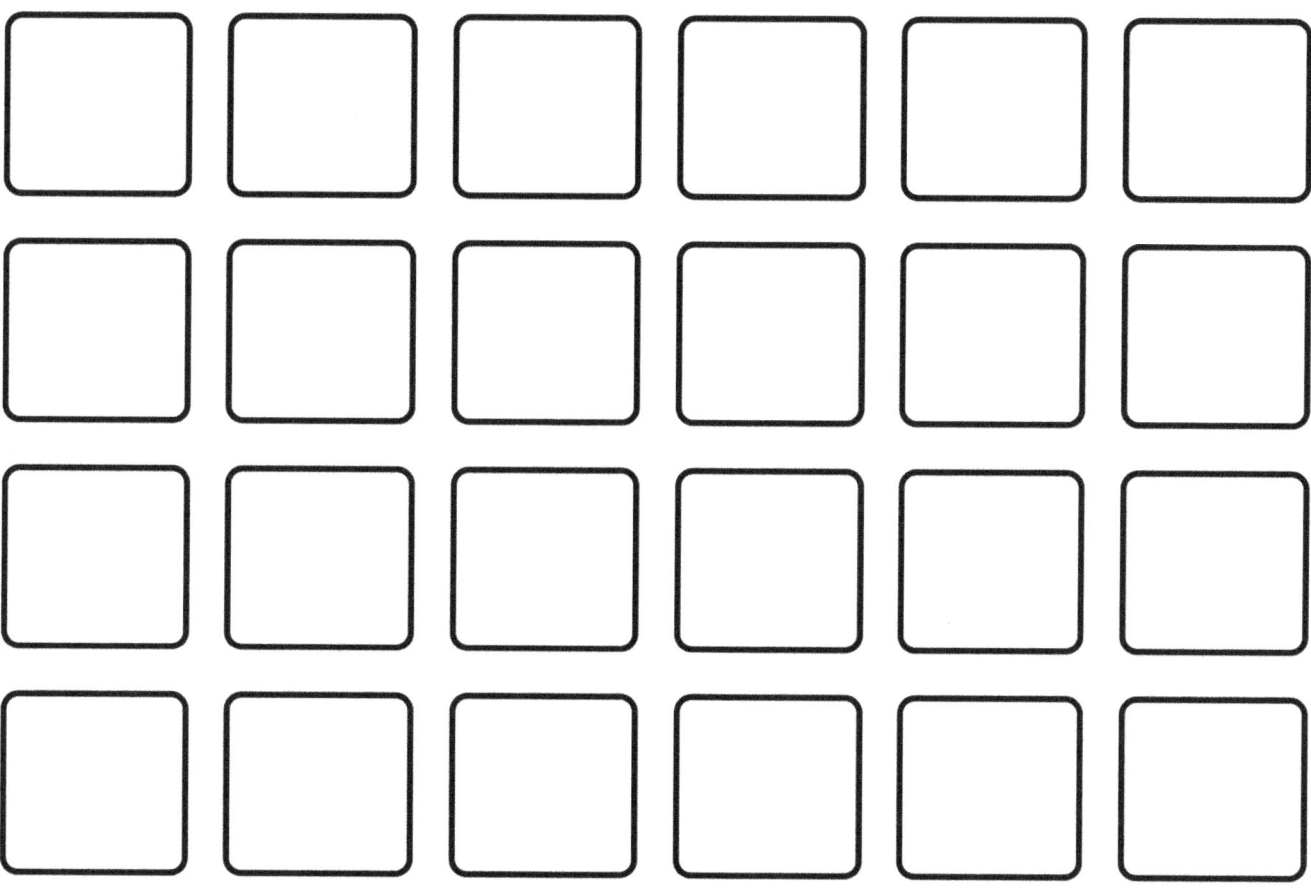

Contents

Introduction 1

Sunlight 3

Twilight 19

Midnight 35

Abyss 51

Conclusion 67

Acknowledgements 68

Contact 68

Introduction

I frequently start my day by reviewing some of my simplest inspirational quotes:

"Always do your best"—Don Miguel Ruiz
"Everything is always working out for me" —Esther Hicks
"Don't be a miserable cow" —someone on the internet

For several years, the pressure and chaos of my day-to-day life left me feeling overwhelmed, anxious, and at times, indifferent. Often, when I got a moment to relax, the time I spent unwinding went into numbing out the stressful college experience, unfulfilling career, disappointing relationships, or whatever else I had going on at the time. I regularly ended my sessions of indulgence feeling desensitized, uninspired, and dreading the return to reality. What happened after? Rinse and repeat again, and again, and again.

  I know I am not alone in experiencing this turmoil, and from years of cultivating my happiness, I realized that it doesn't have to be this way. We can wake up in the morning inspired to live our lives joyfully, create from the heart, and continuously uplift ourselves and the people around us.

  All we need to do is to tap into the truth that is already inside of us. We already have all the tools we need, we just need to uncover and use them.

  I gradually altered my life by reprogramming my habits, reading and applying knowledge from self-help books, and going on a journey of introspection. This coloring and journaling book is the result of an endless soul-searching process. It will provide a mindful way to unwind from the challenges of the day, as well as introduce you to a variety of journaling prompts to reflect on your life, see what you need to discover about yourself, observe the areas that can use some changes, and position you in the direction which you can grow in to achieve your goals.

To get the most out of this book, set aside some time to tune into yourself with these ocean-inspired sections of journaling prompts and mandala coloring pages. Take a writing utensil and a journal that you feel a loving connection with and set an intention to learn something new about yourself and improve your life in the process. Remember, self-discovery is an infinite journey and you don't have to do everything all at once. A little bit goes a long way, so focus on creating an enchanting, introspective experience, and observe yourself transform.

Sunlight

Description and Intention

The Sunlight Zone of the ocean, which extends to a depth of approximately 660 feet, serves as the inspiration for this section. Just as the surface of the ocean is teeming with life and activity, we will dive into the surface of our own inner worlds. We will examine the topics and issues that are currently surfacing for us and create a safe and nurturing space for them to be explored. Try to set aside at least 30 minutes per question to answer it in depth. These questions will put you in the habit of welcoming whatever you are feeling so that you can further develop self-love and acceptance. In this section, as well as the following ones, you can read responses collected from a diverse group of people on the back of the mandala pages.

Sounds, Scents, and Tea

Create a peaceful environment for exploring the surface of your inner world by listening to cricket sounds, relaxing harp music, and 1111 Hz meditation sounds. The frequency 1111 Hz is known to inspire feelings of happiness, gratitude, and tranquility. To enhance the experience, you may also incorporate scents such as lavender, vanilla, orange, or pine. Also consider brewing yourself a tea made from plants such as mint, rose, or chamomile.

Introspective Journaling

- Reflecting on my daily routine, which are the top five habits that make me feel energized and the top five that drain my energy? How can I make adjustments to my routine by minimizing the draining habits and maximizing the uplifting ones? Are there any new activities or hobbies that I would like to explore that could help restore my energy levels?

- How am I feeling right now? What are three feelings I would like a larger experience of? What small steps can I take to embody those feelings?

- What are my three most important relationships and how are they going? Are each of these relationships serving me and the other person on the deepest possible level? Am I content with where these relationships are at or would I prefer to take them in another direction? Are there any relationships I don't yet have, that I would like to cultivate?

- What was my final thought last night before I fell asleep? What do I usually think about when I fall asleep? Does what I think about at night correlate with how I feel when I wake up in the morning?

I would say that I'm feeling anxious, excited, determined, empowered, and concerned currently I'm pretty happy with this, and I would love to feel more genuine trust in myself, calm, and focus. I believe embodying those feelings comes down to sitting with myself. Quieting my mind, letting it take a break. I can also simply breathe deeply no matter what I'm doing; slow deep Yin breathing to help my entire nervous system to feel calm. I'm doing it as I write, which is already shifting my sense of calm. I also like to look into the mirror and practice loving myself. Sometimes, simply taking a break to be with me helps me cultivate those feelings of trust. There's nothing outside myself that is more powerful than what's inside of me. I can practice reminding myself that every day. Perhaps I'll write a song about it to sing to myself throughout the day. My little mantra. "Trust. Trust. Trust. It's within my heart. Peace, calm, and focus are mine from the start."

Ember, 35

Almost always, dreams I have will be combined with experiences and people I have interacted with throughout and thought of throughout the day. In the case below, I remember who was in my dream and the song that gave it flavor. I don't remember that actions that occurred in the dream now. However, when I first woke up at 7:30am this morning I remembered the dream in clearer detail. I suspect my experiences in remembering dreams are not unique. In the following paragraphs I will attempt to reconstruct my dream.

My final thought last night was about my brother, Joseph, visiting me in Seattle from Washington DC. This was combined with the country song "Last Night" by Morgan Wallen which I have been listening to frequently. I enjoy his accent, he is from Tennessee, as well as his dialect. One phrase I haven't heard since I studied abroad in Querétaro, Mexico is "let the liquor talk". One of the joys of studying abroad is that one gets to meet people from all over the world who are also abroad, in addition to exposure to people from various regions. In this case, Tim was from rural southern Illinois. He was the first person I remember using the phrase, "let the liquor talk". I assume that I combined "let the liquor talk" with my brother coming home but I don't remember how. I do know that the song by Morgan Wallen sings about a couple fighting while drunk and saying things they don't mean, letting the liquor talk, the assumption by the singer is that although they have argued that is not the end of the relationship.

Upon reflection, I remember my brother mentioning that he would see his girlfriend, Elena, when he arrived. That was probably combined with the song's sense of something being amiss when a couple was not in the same place. Additionally, I remember bucolic country scenes in my dream and chatting with the two of them happily. The atmosphere of my dream was not sinister which suggests something was coming right rather than amiss. When I woke up today, I felt happy knowing I would see my brother soon. I feel satisfied in how I reconstructed my dream and happy to have been able to label it a good dream!

Andrew, 35

Last night before I fell asleep I was up late thinking about all the work I need to complete by the end of the week. Within these thoughts were pot holes of self-doubt, anxiety and self-disappointment, as I was not happy with the amount of work I had completed that day, despite working long hours the days before. I struggled to navigate around them but just accepted they were there living inside my head. When I closed my eyes I was submerged with dramatized visions of situations and outcomes which rationally would not happen or come true.

On most nights when I cannot seem to calm the fires of my thoughts, I often find myself like Alice thinking of ten impossible thoughts before bedtime: a dragon with no teeth, a cat with webbed feet, otters that can fly with wings. If my brain wants to overthink on its own, I will give it something better to think about. Waking in the morning after a bedtime full of impossible things, I find myself feeling energized and more relaxed as I have not spent the night stressing about work I need to get done.

The energized feeling helps to pull myself from my bed and gives me the energy to complete the work I need to do, while in turn helps me not feel guilty about taking breaks throughout the day.

Bayley, 20

In the evening before I sleep, I recently started to recall everything I had done that day. Among them are the events at school, the things I talked about with my friends, and my thoughts throughout the day. It helps me feel more organized and prepared the next day. This process also helps me clear my mind before going to sleep. I can address any lingering thoughts or worries so that I can have a more restful sleep. During this time, I also sometimes like to contemplate my next goals and aspirations. It helps me figure out what my next steps are and what actions I have to take to get closer to them.

I'd also like to think that this habit of reflection helps me not only stay more organized but also help me learn from my experiences. When I look over my actions that day, I can think about what to improve on.

I especially like predicting what could happen the next day based on what happened today. It's pretty easy once you do it for a few days—it almost makes me feel like a detective, finding little clues and hints that can give me a sense of what's to come.

I hope to make this a part of my daily routine before I go to sleep. I think it would really help me with personal growth and clarity of mind.

Sonja, 15

I begin my daily routine by reflecting on my goals. I lay and watch my mind begin to hum, observing the feelings and thoughts that first come up. Then I clear my mind and energies. I meditate on how I want my day to feel like, and then I choose any thoughts or feelings that align. I start to make some minor goals like what to make for dinner, what to learn about, and any responsibilities I may need to address throughout the new day. After 15 to 30 mins of meditation, I drink at least 2 large glasses of water. When I'm feeling especially inspired, I jump into a cold shower for a few minutes to shock my mind and body into alertness and aliveness. This is a powerful tool to wake up and get in the right mindset for the day. I remind myself that I can choose to feel how I want to feel, and I choose the most positive feelings I can. I find it especially energizing to find an interesting playlist of my favorite songs or genre of music while I shower. The music helps to get my mind off the cold and to direct my focus into my heart. In other words these five activities energize me the most: reflection, meditation, hydration, cold water immersion, and vibing to good music.

Joseph, 27

Five habits that drain my energy is looking at screens towards the evening, not getting enough sleep, not eating breakfast lunch or dinner at all or on time, and not planning stuff out.

Five things which help me feel energized is getting my full 8 hours of slumber, going to bed early, having a quick (maybe light) breakfast, starting the day early in general, and getting many things done towards the beginning of the day. A cold shower gives that mental and physical boost as well.

I know I need to stretch more, so I should do an hour of that before bed while listening to music or praying or something which will ready me for bed would be smart. It would decrease injury as well as increase my sleep quality. Fixing two huge drags in my life. If I fix this, it would provide so much higher quality work during the day. The pros would be so high to the relatively small sacrifice I need to make. I've done this before and it felt like I was cheating at life. Yes, it's hard, but if we go all in, and we're alive so we're all in anyways, then might as well play the best hand possible.

Anthony, 21

My three most important relationships are with:

- Myself—this one is going ok, could be better. I have a healthy amount of self-love and I am working on showing up for myself, keeping promises to myself, and getting comfortable with the uncomfortable.
- My partner—it's as good as it could be. I am content. It was very magical at the start but now the spark has faded. Despite the hours of conversations to resolve our issues, we never seem to see eye to eye on them for very long. I do wonder if there is someone out there who is more compatible for me or would I inevitably be disappointed with anyone I end up dating.
- The world around me—it's easy to feel like an outsider, to feel like I am alone in what I am going through. But I know that everybody is trying to figure it out. There are no rules. There is no one right answer. We are all just guessing our best and so I try to relate to every person in that way.

I try to maintain my relationships in a way that benefits everyone who is involved in them. Something to note about my romantic relationship is the beauty of serving each other. When we are in service to each other, life is beautiful.

Maggie, 29

Twilight

Description and Intention

The next zone of the ocean is called the Twilight Zone, and it reaches down to around 3300 feet. This area of the ocean starts to become home to bioluminescent creatures. In this section we'll explore our own inner light in relation to our darkness. It is important to befriend our darkness as well as our light so that we can gain a deeper understanding of subconscious thoughts, emotions, and behaviors that may have been repressed or ignored. By acknowledging and embracing these aspects, we can become more self-aware and reduce internal conflict, leading to more harmonious relationships and fulfilling personal growth. Understanding and accepting your shadows and light can help you become more accepting and empathetic towards others and reduce judgment and negativity. Try to spend at least an hour on the journaling questions in this section to gain the deepest understanding of these internal aspects of yourself.

Sounds, Scents, and Tea

Enhance the experience of diving below the surface by listening to forest sounds, rain sounds, and 999 Hz frequency. Playing 999 Hz sounds can encourage fluidity, insight, harmony, and serenity. Explore the scents of mint, sage, eucalyptus and rosemary. Make some tea such as rooibos, chai, or oolong.

Introspective Journaling

- Consider all the things you aspire to attain in life and record them. Reflect on your list and vividly imagine yourself achieving each one. In addition, observe your emotions as you come to each individual item.

- Am I motivated by avoidance or attraction when it comes to my desires? Am I striving to achieve these things as a way to escape something or am I working towards them because they truly align with my values and passions? *This can be determined by observing your emotions towards your goal. Are you feeling expansion and joy when you think of it? That is an indication that you are in alignment with it. If you experience feelings of tightness, fear, or insecurity, this is an invitation to explore possible limiting beliefs you may have around that subject and reexamine it as a worthwhile pursuit.*

- How do I feel about my body? Which parts of my body do I love? Which parts of my body can I give more love and light to?

- What are my negative self-talk patterns? How do they affect my confidence, well-being, and self-esteem?

Every day I sing a little song with my ukulele, making up a spell of this picture of my life.

   I picture myself sitting on the deck of my mountain property, watching the sunrise while I drink my morning ceremonial cacao. I watch my son with curly hair running around, being free and expressive, playing with the dog. I picture my partner sitting next to me. I envision inviting my friends and those who need healing to my property. I envision myself being free and dancing with my partner to the music we both write. I see the faces of the people who come to visit me there and I feel their love and their anticipation at what it will be like to heal and to transform through their body and voice. I picture myself leading them in ceremonies, exercises, and individual sessions.

   I picture myself directing a team of people to take care of tasks that allow me to do my work well and I embody the feeling of being excited that I have so many people contributing to my work, and my partner's work, of helping others heal and step into a higher vibration. I also picture myself singing, creating intuitive music and joyfully celebrating through song, incorporating what I love. Perhaps even hosting retreats where others lead, using my skills as a hostess to create the most amazing experience for my friends and family.

   When I picture all of this, and the places I'll be doing it from, I feel aligned. There's many paths my life has started down, all of these little divergences in the woods. I've followed many less traveled paths, only to discover that they end. This doesn't feel like an ending. It feels like a continuation of my story, of my family's story, of humanity. It truly feels like home. I'm a bit emotional thinking about it. I know there will be many sacrifices, but there will also be so much joy and fulfillment. I saw this life as a child, before I was given other choices and paths that people said might be better for me. I sing my little song as a way of choosing this path every day.

Ember, 35

I used to be a wrestler in high school. When you're 16 years old and wrestling, it's very difficult to be fat. We used to work out 6 times a week. In the morning, it was an hour of weight training, and after school it was 2 hours of grueling practice. When you're a boy going through puberty and training all the time, you can get away with eating a lot of food. I used to get into fights with my mom because she would buy a gallon of milk, and I would just drink the entire thing in a day.

    This changed when I went to college. I gained weight. A lot of it. During my sophomore year of college I weighed 220lbs at 5'9. People treat you differently when you're fat. Dating is a lot harder because people don't find you attractive. It happens gradually, so you almost don't notice it until you do. Girls no longer smile at you when you're walking past them, and you become more and more invisible.

    The thing that people don't tell you about being fat though is that it isn't just the opposite sex that treats you differently. It's everybody. People no longer care as much about your opinions, even if it has nothing to do with health or looks. They talk over you when you have something to say. I remember having technical discussions about a physics problem in a study group in college, and not being taken seriously even though I was objectively in the right. I thought this was just reality.

    I've lost 60lbs since my heaviest. I started working out again and watching what I eat. I'm a lot leaner and more muscular than I was before. I'm a lot more comfortable wearing clothes that aren't oversized. People automatically assume good things about me now. As if getting fit somehow changed the person that I am. When I tell people I used to be fat and started working out, the automatic assumption is that it was because I wanted to get more attention from girls. This is only a fraction of the truth. When you get fit, you get a lot more attention from straight men. A lot more. Only other men care about the size of your quads or the veins on your forearms. Men are less aggressive towards/more intimidated by you and treat you with more respect. It's a strange dynamic.

Alex, 27

Sometimes when I lie awake at night and reflect on the day, I realize that the thoughts I bury deepest within myself are regret and disappointment. Why didn't I do more in the day? I could have completed that if I had managed my time better. I should have spent more time with my loved ones making memories instead of wasting my time on things that only draw me away from them. Why do I procrastinate? Why am I scared of starting something new, and why do I avoid finishing something old? Why do I spend my time in an endless loop where nothing is gained and is only lost?

I suppose that introspection like this can be a blessing and a curse, where endlessly thinking about the things I could have done can end up costing even more time. Where I beat myself down about what could have been or should have been, instead of focusing on what has been. This way of talking to myself, belittling my actions, only serves to tear my self-confidence, self-esteem, and self-image down.

Crystalizing my thoughts on paper helps me to confront myself. If I choose to care for others and love them, then my own self is deserving of that love too. When I choose to be my own loyal supporter, something changes and I start to notice all that I do is not a waste. The times in the day where I reach out to an old friend to check up on them to let them know I care. The times when I don't complete all my tasks, but I still manage to do more than enough. When I enjoy the small pleasures in the day, and it gives me more energy to keep going. When I treat myself gently by writing small encouraging notes to saying "You can do it", "One small step at a time", "Take a deep breath", "You won't sink", "I promise you can get through this", "I believe in you", and "You did the best you could".

I manage to achieve the greatest things when I love myself the way I love others. At the end of the day when I shut my eyes to sleep, I've finished a beautiful page that did not exist before, and would never have existed without me. I only need to do better than I did yesterday, and I'm sure I will create something new tomorrow. Something beautiful.

Samantha, 26

I try my best to love my body. Some days are better than others. I realize what areas I can improve in ways that I consider valuable, but I learned a long time ago that the only one whose opinion truly matters when it comes to our self-image is ourselves.

I appreciate my smile, the joyful lines around my eyes, and I consider my wrinkles to be marks of character. I could be more kind to parts of my face and to my legs. I've always struggled to view my body positively, and I celebrate every step I've taken along the way to get to where I am now. Positive self-talk has been the key to the change in my self-esteem, and mindfulness has been the key to acknowledging and letting go of the intrusive negative thoughts that used to preoccupy my mind.

Before I graduated high school, I told myself some pretty horrible things. I would look at myself in the mirror and blame myself for my poor appearance. My behavior was a reflection of the beliefs I developed after years and years of this toxic internal monologue. I felt like my own mind was a prison of demoralizing, demeaning, and unkind messaging that kept me trapped in my flaws.

I decided to change one day in college and promise myself to smile kindly in the mirror every morning and to greet every single person with whom I made eye contact with. I greeted everyone on my walk to and from work, in the store, and in public, except in situations where my attention was required. A simple hello or hi, a casual remark about the weather, a friendly joke or a compliment, or even a simple expression was the goal. And I promised to give myself a few minutes every morning to intentionally say supportive, inspiring, and encouraging statements to myself.

This dramatically improved my quality of life, unlocked the space for constructive transformation to occur, and I've never gone back to ruminating over negative internal monologues or self-concepts that don't serve me or represent self-love.

Joseph, 27

In the past few months, I have been feeling very much more insecure about my body and face. I guess it's the age. I've reached the age where science and people tell me things like my "peak" is over, my look "could crash at any time", I could look very different overnight, my metabolism is down no matter how much I try, etc.

Now, when anything happens to how I look, like gaining weight, I panic. I've always liked my breasts, probably because people told me that too. Now I keep thinking if one day they will just be saggy. All the things I don't like about my body, I don't know what they will become. And how will I feel about them if that happens? Will I be fine with it, or be sad for years till I finally accept it or inevitably get used to it?

I keep telling myself that all those theories are just conjecture, that we can always make a change if we try hard enough. But I can't convince myself. Then I keep telling myself aging is fine. Obviously, I can't convince myself either. I remember before I turned 30 I was scared, but then I felt perfectly fine the moment I hit that number.

Maybe what's unknown is always the scariest thing. Maybe I will always find a way to adapt when it happens. I hope so. If there's one part of my body I want to empower, I guess it's my mind and mentality.

Eivee, 35

I don't like my current job. And I'm dying to change that. I know I'm never brave enough to just quit the job and focus on finding a new job, which might give me more motivation/pressure to do so.

Last year I told myself that I would start looking as soon as my last big project was done. Now almost 4 months have passed, and I haven't started looking. Yes, work has been hectic and I don't have much time. But is that really why? Do I need to socialize so much with how little time I have outside work? I could use that time to work on my resume. Was I avoiding it because I'm procrastinating or not motivated enough? Then I remember when sometimes I browsed the jobs on the email alerts that I had set on LinkedIn and some other job sites, I was like: Will this be better than my current job? Will I like it better? Then it leads to a bigger question that I fear: What do I like?

That's where I stopped looking and went down a rabbit hole of existential crisis. I guess I have a general idea of what I want in an ideal job, but can any job be like that ALL THE TIME? I have ups and downs in my current job, will that be the case in my next one? So, do I want a new job only because I want to run away from this one? Do I want something simply because I don't like what I have? I reasoned with myself a lot about this. Now I am aware that I'm more often motivated by "I don't want this" than "I want that". But I also convinced myself that it's not a bad thing. Nothing is perfect, then what harm is in ditching the one I know I don't like and being open to maybe another mistake? It might apply to everything in my life too. At least that's what I keep telling myself now when I let myself hesitate again. Whatever motivation it is, that's better than no motivation, I guess?

Eivee, 35

Things I aspire to do and attain in life:

- radical growth, always leveling up
- publishing a book
- body awareness and amazing mobility
- running a successful business
- traveling to many different places
- raising kids with a supportive partner
- eating delicious food from around the world
- starting every day with peaceful morning rituals
- enjoying thrilling, wild, mind-blowing adventures with my ride or die
- going on a spiritually connected girls trip with my best friends
- meeting different people, learning their stories, serving them, and co-creating with them
- dancing to my heart's content
- having a peaceful home I can relax in
- enjoying life as a housewife
- surrendering

Some of these things bring up feelings of joy and excitement. Others bring up tightness and resentment. I don't know what life has in store for me. I hope to always do my best to stay grateful.

Jessica, 26

Midnight

Description and Intention

The Midnight Zone of the ocean goes down to around 13,000 feet. This area of the ocean does not receive any sunlight at all. Similarly, we will explore the depths of our inner world that may not have been illuminated before. Uncovering parts of ourselves we may not know about can empower us by providing new tools to face challenges with. Try to answer the journaling prompts in this section every month and see how your answers change as time goes on.

Sounds, Scents, and Tea

Sink into a meditative experience by listening to cat purrs, 741 Hz, and 528 Hz sounds. The frequency 741 Hz helps to unite our mind, body, and environment, while 528 Hz sounds facilitate grounding, acceptance, and surrendering to your experience. Surround yourself with incense, candles, or different essential oils containing jasmine, angelica root, rose, and lemon. Sip on tea blends like earl grey, nettle or lavender to stimulate your taste buds.

Introspective Journaling

- Which habits, thoughts, relationships, or possessions are holding me back from happiness? What specific things or patterns in my life are no longer serving me? What would be the benefits of letting go of them and how can I replace them with something that will serve me better?

- What are some situations where I felt ashamed, embarrassed, or guilty? What are the thoughts, feelings, and bodily sensations coming up for me when I think about these things? How can I meet this feeling in a loving and accepting way?

- If I sit still and bring awareness to my body, where do I feel tension or stuck energy? Does it present itself in tightness, pain, discomfort? How does it affect my overall well-being and what emotions are associated with it? What regular practice can I do to release it?

- What were some experiences in my life where I felt vulnerable? Do I see vulnerability as good or bad? What are the benefits and drawbacks of being open and vulnerable?

One of the most difficult, shameful and embarrassing situations I often find myself in is my architectural crit/reviews at university. Presenting my work at the beginning or halfway through a project, when most of my designs and concepts are still on tracing paper, and contain rough diagrams thrown together on photoshop, the thoughts of anxiety, dread, embarrassment, and stupidity make my body freeze up for a single moment, and I start belittle myself, and think I am not good enough.

   To match this feeling in the opposite, and turn a negative emotion or feeling into a positive, loving and accepting one, I remind myself of all the achievements I have accomplished as well as reminding myself that I have my own design process that I know works for me. To help break the ice freeze I find myself in, I have, as of recent, started to surround my work with love. In particular, the parts of my work that I do not like. I will think positively of the work I have produced and know it will only get better with time and acceptance of self-love.

                                          Bayley, 20

I feel discomfort and stress on my skin and in my gut. Naturally I am an anxious person and I have spent countless hours of my life worrying. I also have an autoimmune disease. If I experience a level of anxiety, the stress will physically manifest itself into a flare-up for me. This is a hard cycle to break because when my health is poor I become even more tense.

A tactic I have is to focus on my breath. I will "convert" all of my tense energy into breathing deep, slow breaths until I sense that some clarity has returned. Sometimes when it is too much to bear, and I have the luxury of isolation, I will have a good cry. Screaming into my pillow or throwing on headphones and blasting music is extremely cathartic. If I don't have the luxury of being alone, then I will make it happen by taking a walk. It is usually better when I get the chance to walk outside in the fresh air. I will keep walking until I feel calm again.

Often when I'm stressed however, I spiral into self-hatred and imposter syndrome. I begin to doubt my accomplishments. I look at myself in the mirror in disgust. It is a horrible moment. I have found that the best ways for me to move through the stress is to break a sweat with exercise, talk to somebody about my feelings, or finish the task I've been avoiding.

If I feel anxious and cannot pinpoint what is bothering me, the best way to push through the uncertainty is movement. Recently I started pole dancing. For years I wanted to make dance my hobby but I let excuses get in my way. I am only a week into pole, but I'm so excited to continue. I figure that if I pour more of my energy into good things, then I will have less energy to worry.

Lumi, 25

I was part of a non-religious, spiritual church for a while growing up and stayed in touch with the youth group as we transitioned into young adulthood. Opportunities offered for young adults included these weekend long camps called cons. I remember hearing about one when I was about 20 in Sacramento, two states away. I would know about two people there at most from prior events.

I remember thinking "what am I doing" when I got off the plane and got on the bus to the college that the camp was close to. I took the wrong bus and ended up circling around the city twice. Best of all, I had all this glitter in my hair that kept getting on everything. It took me so much courage to order an Uber to the church the camp was held at. The driver saw I was visibly nervous, so much I could barely utter out the words to explain where we were going, and so he had to make me laugh the whole time.

I went in and had a weekend I loved. I made new friends, connected with old ones, heard some of the most room silencing, chill producing musical performances by members there, and it felt like I had come home after a long, long time away. There was virtually no social hierarchy, probably since most were radical, self-proclaimed hippies. Expectations such as gender norms, heteronormativity, and personal expression were dismantled, along with the social and political theory behind them.

I had to rethink all of this. The benefit I see to being vulnerable is that it's difficult to have a closed mind for too long, which is why I think vulnerability is powerful. Another benefit is the sheer excitement, which I believe adults need more of. You also get to learn what's right and what's wrong (and what's in between) for yourself more clearly through different situations, people, trajectories.

A drawback is that it's possible to feel lost at first like I literally was on the bus ride there. Currently, the camps are postponed due to Covid and haven't yet started back up, but I can still see that dim light in the rearview mirror.

Emily, 23

The main thing holding me back from happiness is the man in the mirror. Every day, I know I can do more but I am so afraid to fail, I make excuses to not push myself and take risks. I grew up not being allowed to fail (there's another excuse) and I don't have experience with failure. Which often prevents me from taking action. I want so badly to take enough action just so I can indeed fail. Just to experience having done something meaningful.

                                                                          Frank, 19

Most recently, I have been educating myself on the wisdom of our physical bodies and how the mind affects the body. How a lot of physical conditions and ailments are caused by external factors.

With that knowledge, I have been able to heal my own pains, rashes, headaches, stomach aches, pulled muscles, tooth aches, and other problems without the help of doctors or medications. I do it by evaluating and correcting things in my life that are not serving me, eating intuitively and mindfully, honoring and supporting my body's cyclical nature, practicing gratitude, and sending love to the affected painful area.

If I sit still and bring awareness to my body, I feel tension and tightness in my jaw. I hold my stress in my jaw. Several year ago, I used to hold my stress in my pelvic floor. It got so bad that I was in pain 24/7 for multiple months. Sex hurt, walking hurt. And it was a self-feeding monster. The more anxious I felt, the more my body responded with pain. The more pain I felt, the more anxious I became. Having over 10 doctors over 4 years examine me, do various tests, prescribe multiple medications, and tell me that nothing is wrong with me didn't help.

Finally, a physical therapist helped me to learn to relax my pelvic floor muscles. I learned that the pain was coming from the anxiety I was experiencing from my job and unresolved childhood trauma. It gave me a little humor to be able to joke about my very real "crippling anxiety." I know I can do the same for my jaw. Cause my face hurts all the time, ouch!

I will work on identifying my stress the moment that it happens (because sometimes I swim in it and don't realize I am letting myself get swept up by its current) and surrendering to the experience. I will let the stressful situation move through me physically, emotionally, spiritually. That's the goal anyways.

Avery, 28

One of the most significant experiences that come to mind where I've felt ashamed, embarrassed, or guilty, was losing my job a few years ago. I remember feeling like a failure and being too ashamed to share with my extended family that I was unemployed.

When I reflect on this experience, it brings up negative and self-critical thoughts. I worried about how my job loss would impact my future and it felt like I let myself and my family down. I also felt sad, anxious, and unworthy. My body responded by feeling tense, and I experienced sensations like a tightness in my chest and indigestion in my stomach.

To approach these feelings in a loving and accepting way, I reminded myself that it's normal to feel ashamed, embarrassed, or guilty in the face of adversity. I practiced self-compassion by speaking to myself kindly and understandingly, just like I would with a good friend who is going through a tough time.

I continue to focus on my positive qualities and strengths, even in the face of hardships. I think about the things I'm grateful for in my life and work on building my resilience and self-confidence. Lastly, I seek support from my spouse and close friends to help me process these challenging emotions and develop a more positive outlook on life.

Mike, 40

One experience that stands out to me as vulnerable, new, and out of my comfort zone, was when I traveled solo to a foreign country for the first time. I was excited to explore and immerse myself in a new culture, but I was also nervous and scared of being, robbed, assaulted, trafficked, and murdered.

As I navigated the new environment, I found myself feeling uneasy and unsure of myself at times. I had to learn to rely on my instincts, communicate with strangers who spoke a different language, and be brave enough to try new things. While it was challenging, it was also a transformative experience that helped me grow and learn more about myself.

Reflecting on this experience, I see vulnerability as a good thing. It allows me to be open to new experiences, learn from others, and grow as a person. However, I also recognize that vulnerability can have its drawbacks. It can make me feel exposed and uncomfortable, and there's always the risk of getting hurt or rejected.

Despite the potential drawbacks, I believe that being open and vulnerable is worth it. It allows me to build stronger connections with others, be authentic, and live a more fulfilling life. I've learned that vulnerability is not a weakness, but rather a strength that requires courage and resilience.

Every time that being vulnerable brought about "failure" (i.e. I ended up being hurt, crushed, heartbroken, betrayed), I learned valuable lessons and came out better, stronger, smarter, sexier, kinder, wittier, and more powerful on the other side. Of course, while you're in the middle of a crisis, it never feels good. It often doesn't feel like there's a greater purpose to the struggle. But historically for me, there has always been a reward for overcoming a challenge, and that is what keeps me going through the really tough challenges.

Marianne, 38

Abyss

Description and Intention

The ocean zone known as the Abyss is nearly 20,000 feet below the surface of the Earth. This area is known for its vastness and extreme pressure conditions. In this section, we will delve deeply into ourselves to explore territories that are yet to be charted for us. Uncovering the truth of our core opens us up to new experiences and expansion. Consider sharing your journaling responses with others to co-create a deeply connecting and mindful conversation. Being open and vulnerable with others brings forth evolution of our souls in the universe.

Sounds, Scents, and Tea

Align with regeneration and well-being as you sink into the abyss with 111 Hz and 432 Hz sounds. Synchronicity with the universe can be tapped into through these frequencies. Surround yourself with sandalwood, cedar, geranium, and lotus scents to expand your olfactory senses, and enjoy tea made with matcha, lemon ginger, or hibiscus to enhance the overall experience.

Introspective Journaling

- Where is my fear focused today? How can I befriend my fear and let it teach me something about myself? Does fear motivate me or hold me back? Do I experience different types of fear?

- How has my definition of success changed over time? Why has it changed? What did it mean before and what does it mean now?

- Considering my experiences, upbringing, personality, beliefs, values, skills, and talents, what are the top five core parts of my identity? How attached am I to each of these parts? In what situations are they beneficial, harmful, or neutral? Are any parts of my identity home to limiting beliefs?

- What does happiness mean to me? Why is that my definition of happiness? By my definition, am I happy? Are there certain aspects of my life that I am happier about more than other aspects? Am I feeling a sense of gratitude and appreciation for the happiness that I already have in my life?

Last month I decided to start keeping a fear journal so that I could learn to face my fears better. The journal was in the form of a table with the following columns: *Date, Description of Fear, Did I do it?*, and *Result*. Every time I was afraid of doing something, I logged my fear and how doing or not doing the thing I was afraid of made me feel afterwards. I learned that I experience two different types of fear. One type of fear holds me back from opportunities, and the other protects me from danger.

An example of the first fear was being afraid to talk to people at a meetup. I am a huge introvert and talking to people can be very scary, especially initial introductions. I forced myself to do it at the meetup event and pleasantly, as the night went on, it got easier for me to be able to talk to people. Facing my fear made me feel brave and more empowered, as well as giving me confidence that I can do it again in the future and in other situations. This type of fear is very good to face.

The second type of fear that I faced was very tricky and akin to caution. It's the type of fear that is an uneasy gut feeling about a potentially unsafe stranger, the hyperawareness fear of walking home alone in the dark, and the suspicion of a loved one lying to you. It is not obvious how to even face this type of fear without putting yourself into physical or emotional danger. The best option I came up with so far is listening to my instincts very intuitively to decide if this is a situation I can get hurt in or it's a situation I can grow from if I face my fear. I don't think this is a perfect solution.

I even wonder if these two types of fear are actually the same type of fear with different outcomes. Maybe my brain is always trying to protect me from danger and things that seem out of my comfort zone just feel dangerous to my brain?

Cora, 27

I can say that my definition of success has changed significantly over the years. When I was younger, success was all about achieving financial stability, sleeping with a lot of women, chasing professional success, and getting the approval of my friends.

However, as I grew older and gained more life experience, my definition of success shifted towards more internal factors. I realized that true success is not just about how much money I make or how high I climb the corporate ladder, but it's also about finding purpose and meaning in my life, and making a positive impact on others.

Now, success to me means being able to live a balanced and fulfilling life that includes not just work, but also family, friends, and personal interests. It means being able to pursue my passions and hobbies, and finding joy in the simple things in life.

I also place a greater emphasis on making a positive impact on others and giving back to my community. Success to me now means using my skills and resources to help others and make the world a better place.

In summary, my definition of success has changed over time from being externally focused on financial and professional success to being more internally focused on personal growth, relationships, and making a positive impact on others.

Garrett, 42

My top five core identities are considered to be the ability of staying alone and independent, the ability of adaptation, the ability of accepting change, the tendency of escape, and the ability of trying something new.

   I think I am pretty attached to all of them. Sometimes I wish I can escape from the life I don't like, so I keep changing, and that could really harm me in terms of the lack of stability.

   I am still on the road of finding myself.

Taco, 32

The following core parts are equally attached to my identity:

Family-oriented (value): Growing up in an immigrant single-parent Vietnamese household, family is essential to our cultural beliefs. I instill familial piety in many of my life's decisions, however, it has caused a lot of pain, heartache, and disappointment when I cannot let go of those who hurt me. I fantasize that I can fix the people I love, and make up for all their mistakes, traumas, and flaws. In the end, I am the one that is left defeated, exhausted, and all alone. Essentially, I am the one who created my own hell because I chose to hold onto hurt people who hurt others.

Empathetic/sympathetic/considerate of others (personality): Growing up with an unstable childhood, I am highly sensitive to others' emotions and state of being. It is a defense mechanism I possess to ensure my own safety. Being able to adjust accordingly to the environment around me allows me to protect myself and subdue others' negative emotions (aggression, anger, despair, and resentment). Other people's negative emotions trigger my anxiety, create fear, and build apprehension in me. I do love the fact that I can care for others, sympathize with how they are feeling, and notice those that do not wish to be seen, but it is hard to continuously give to others when my own cup is empty. I am harming myself because I disregard my own well-being to maintain peace in others. I lead with my heart, but I get hurt in the process.

Strong-willed (upbringing): My childhood has been stolen from me. I have learned to mature at a young age. I am highly independent, mistrustful of others, and hyperaware. I have faced familial, financial, and societal adversities. Although I am proud of who I am, it is a double-edged sword. As a female, I walk in my masculine energy, I do not easily let others in, I possess hidden resentment, and am angry at the world for being unfair and cruel to me.

From one stranger to another: I hope sharing my experiences, thoughts, and transparency will help you in your own journey. Know that you are not alone. I am right by your side. Celebrating both your downfalls and your success.

JMN, 23

Happiness could mean different things to different stages of my life. I don't have any deep insight into how I can achieve happiness. All I can do is to list out the things that have made me happy:

- Doing a good job at whatever I do and being proud of the work I have done
- Helping my family out of a tight spot
- After a hard day at work, having time to relax and self-reflect
- Going for a walk after a productive day at work
- Morning sunshine, coffee, and café music
- Cuddling and watching an enjoyable show with my loved ones
- Playing guitar and singing with my friends
- Dancing to a really good song and being in the moment
- Playing with cute dogs who love me
- Organizing my room and making it tidy and neat
- Having all my businesses in order
- Having a thought-provoking chat with someone who I admire
- Consulting or teaching
- Growth e.g. learn new skills and being able to do what I couldn't before
- Working on cool projects, doing amazing things with amazing people
- Making someone's day better, specifically someone I care about, like a dear friend
- Falling asleep with my love in my arms

Rufus, 35

Happiness to me means feeling a sense of ease and comfort in my day to day life. It means having someone to love, something to do, and something to look forward to. I believe that happiness includes feeling a range of emotions, even ones that are typically defined as negative, because that is part of the human experience. I also believe that happiness comes from the emotion you feel most often, which for me happens to be a feeling of contentedness. Personally, I can have something to do, someone to love, and something to look forward to but if I don't engage with my emotions frequently then I tend to miss the positive moments and emotions that I could be experiencing if I just checked in with myself.

By my definition, I would say I am happy, although writing that feels strange because I feel discontent in many aspects of my life. But of course, saying "engage with your emotions" is easier said than done, so I have a hunch that fear is holding me back from being truly happy. Fear that I will try my best and fail, fear that I will be judged if I engage in the things that make me happy, and fear that those around me won't want to continue being around me if I change.

I haven't quite figured out how to overcome the fear besides using opposite action and diving into the deep end. That's a whole journey within itself. Personally, I feel happiest when I am in the company of those that I love because it feels safe but I struggle to feel happy when I am alone. I try my best to go into each day with a sense of gratitude for all that I do have because I believe gratitude is a core component of happiness.

I think part of happiness is looking at the little things that you can be grateful for while looking at the big picture and seeing how you feel overall. There's a balance and well, balance is hard.

Sage, 27

Happiness means different things to different people. For me, happiness is about the way I feel at the present moment. It means being able to wake up every morning feeling excited about the day ahead. It means staying grateful and present in any moment, regardless if it is a traditionally "positive" or "negative" experience. Life is always going to be full of ups and downs. If we surrender to every experience, we can be happy at any time.

Growing up, my parents taught me that success was the key to happiness. They forced me to work hard and get perfect grades in school. After I graduated high school, I went to college, got a STEM degree, a high paying job, got the car, got the marriage, got the house. While I do see the value in these things, I don't think they alone were enough to bring true happiness. In fact, I felt empty and bored after I achieved these traditional happiness "landmarks". I had to search deeper in myself to find a more meaningful feeling of happiness.

By my current definition, I would say that I am happy. Despite the enormous challenges I am facing in my life, I find a way to stay present and grateful. I appreciate that I can afford the lifestyle that I have, that my friends and family support me, and that I am in good health.

Overall, I believe that happiness is a journey, not a destination. It's not something that can be achieved overnight, but rather something that we must actively work towards every day. By focusing on the things that truly make us happy and grateful, we can find joy and fulfillment in even the smallest moments of life.

Taylor, 29

Conclusion

One Last Thing

Thank you for coloring, journaling, and reading this far. As a first-time author, you will have my deepest gratitude if you could take a moment to leave a review on Amazon for this book. Your feedback will not only help me improve, but also inspire others to embark on their own journey of self-discovery and reflection through coloring and journaling. Thank you again for your support!

Appreciate Everything

As you complete this coloring book and reflect on the mandalas and ocean-inspired sections, take a moment to appreciate the beauty and tranquility that both the mandalas and the ocean provide. The intricate designs of the mandalas and the vastness of the ocean remind us to take a step back, relax, and appreciate the present moment. The journaling prompts throughout the book have guided you on a journey of self-discovery and reflection. Allow mandalas and the ocean to inspire and rejuvenate you on your personal journey.

Don't stop here

Deeply studying the depths and layers of your inner world is the first step to cultivating happiness. The next step is taking action. To explore actionable journaling, join the Pen Paper Canvas Club for free at www.penpapercanvas.com/ppcclub.

Acknowledgements

Everything I do is made better, more precious, and more meaningful by the love, light, and generosity of the people around me. I would like to express my gratitude to the following people for their knowledge, encouragement, support, ideas, love, check-ins, and inspiration during the creation of this book: Larik, Sasha, Migz, Mom, Dad, Alexis, Joyce, Evelyn, Richard, Laura, Hannah, Fernando, and Dong. A special thank you to Tera, my thoughtful and amazing editor, for her genuine feedback and long-standing friendship.

Contact

Visit us at www.penpapercanvas.com to see and purchase other publications. Contact the author via email at connect@penpapercanvas.com and follow us on Facebook and Instagram @penpapercanvas.

www.ingramcontent.com/pod-product-compliance
Lightning Source LLC
Chambersburg PA
CBHW081253040426
42453CB00014B/2403